Unlocking Your Greatest YOU

Turning Awareness into Power, Living Boldly, and Aligning Values with Mindset and Character

Copyright © 2025 by Joseph G. Motley. All rights reserved.

No part of this publication may be reproduced, distributed, or transmitted in any form or by any means, including photocopying, recording, or other electronic or mechanical methods, without the prior written permission of the publisher, except in the case of brief quotations embodied in critical reviews and certain other noncommercial uses permitted by copyright law.

This book is a work of nonfiction. While every effort has been made to provide accurate and current information at the time of publication, the author and publisher assume no responsibility for errors, omissions, or differing interpretations of the subject matter herein.

ISBN: 978-1-80702-122-1 (Paperback)
ISBN: 978-1-80702-123-8 (Hardcover)

For my wife, my daughters, and my grandchildren.

Always believe in you.

Table of Contents

PREFACE 7

INTRODUCTION 9

PART I: THE AWAKENING 11

    CHAPTER 1: THE FIRST STEP TO YOUR GREATEST YOU 13

    CHAPTER 2: YOUR JOURNEY STARTS NOW 15

    CHAPTER 3: DISCOVERING THE REAL YOU 23

    CHAPTER 4: UNLOCKING YOUR HUMAN POTENTIAL 31

PART II: THE VISION 37

    CHAPTER 5: UNLOCKING YOUR POTENTIAL, INSPIRING POSSIBILITY 39

    CHAPTER 6: THE POWER OF AWARENESS 43

    CHAPTER 7: STEP INTO THE VISION OF YOUR HIGHER SELF 47

    CHAPTER 8: THE CHASE FOR "LIVING THE DREAM" 53

PART III: THE TRANSFORMATION 57

Chapter 9: Unlocking Your Greatest You................................. 59

Chapter 10: The Principle of Individuality 63

Chapter 11: The Principle of Communication............................ 65

Chapter 12: The Principle of Awareness...................................... 71

Chapter 13: The Principle of Accountability 93

Chapter 14: The Principle of Responsibility 97

Chapter 15: The Principle of Expectations 101

PART IV: THE ASCENSION 107

The Principles of the i.C.A.A.R.E. Mindset 109

Chapter 16: Your Greatest You...111

Chapter 17: A Message about Life 119

CONCLUSION 123

Preface

Welcome to the Journey of Becoming

You didn't pick up this book by accident.

There's a voice inside you—a quiet but persistent one—that knows you were made for more. Not just to get by, but to live boldly. Not just to fit in, but to stand out. Not just to succeed by the world's standards, but to thrive in your purpose. We should get uncomfortable with words like average, ordinary, and normal because they put you in predefined boxes.

Unlocking Your Greatest You isn't just another motivational book. It's a wake-up call. It's a mirror. It's a movement.

This book is for those who are tired of living by default and are ready to start living by design. For those who want to stop chasing someone else's dream and start walking in their own destiny. For those who feel that stirring in their soul that says, "There's more in me, and I'm ready to unlock it."

Through stories, principles, and practical tools forged from decades of leadership, coaching, and life experience, Joseph G Motley invites you into a new way of thinking—a higher level of awareness that aligns your mindset and character with the life you were meant to live.

You'll be challenged. You'll be inspired. But more importantly, you'll be changed.

So, take a deep breath, open your heart, and turn the page.

Your greatest self is waiting. Let's unlock it together.

Introduction

There comes a moment in life—a quiet, sometimes uncertain moment—when you realize something deeper is calling you. Not just to achieve more or do more, but to become more. Not in comparison to others, but in alignment with who you were always meant to be.

That's the heartbeat of this book.

Unlocking Your Greatest You isn't just about inspiration. It's about transformation. It's about rediscovering the power that already lives within you—power rooted in the strength of your mindset, the depth of your character, and the values that shape the life you choose to live.

This book was written for those who are tired of simply existing and are ready to live boldly, purposefully, and authentically. It's for the dreamers, the doers, and even the doubters who know there's more within them than the world has seen. It's for those who are ready to not just chase success, but to attract it and define it on their own terms—from the inside out.

Each chapter is a mindset, a shift, a mirror—challenging you to reflect, realign, and rise. Whether you're at the start of your journey or somewhere in the middle, this book meets you where you are and walks with you where you're meant to go.

PART I: THE AWAKENING— IGNITING THE JOURNEY WITHIN

Setting the foundation for self-discovery and intentional living

1

The First Step to Your Greatest You

What if tomorrow didn't feel like just another day, but like a new chance to become the person you were always meant to be?

What if you woke up fired up, ready to take on life—not because it's easy, but because you know you're growing into someone extraordinary?

Imagine this:

You look in the mirror and actually feel proud. Not because you're perfect, but because you're becoming powerful—mentally, emotionally, spiritually. Because you're attracting something real, something that makes your life matter. You have talents. You have dreams. You have something the world hasn't seen yet—you.

So, let me ask you:

- WHAT MAKES YOU UNIQUE?
- IS IT YOUR CREATIVITY? YOUR COURAGE?
- THE WAY YOU MAKE PEOPLE FEEL WHEN YOU WALK IN THE ROOM?
- YOUR PASSION FOR MUSIC, SPORTS, WRITING, HELPING, SOLVING, OR PERHAPS LEADING?

Maybe you don't know yet. That's okay. But what if every single day you started uncovering those hidden gifts? Gifts that were planted deep inside you on purpose—not by accident. Gifts *waiting* for you to believe in them.

Here's the truth most people miss: You don't need to have all the answers right now, and you don't need to pretend to have it all figured out.

You just need to start.

When you begin to move toward your purpose—when you live with intention, passion, and authenticity—*everything changes.*

That's when life becomes more than survival. It becomes meaningful. It becomes impactful. It becomes yours.

You matter. Your voice matters. Your dreams matter. And the way you see yourself? That's the key. Because the moment you start believing in yourself and your potential is the moment the world starts seeing it, too.

Are you ready to discover the greatness inside of you? Because it's already there. And it's time.

2

Your Journey Starts Now

What if the very thing you're meant to do in this world is already whispering to you?

Every time your heart beats faster when you're doing something you love, every time you lose track of time because you're so *into it*, and every time a challenge lights a fire in you instead of fear, that's purpose trying to speak to you.

It doesn't always shout. Sometimes, it's a quiet tug, a spark, a feeling that won't go away. And when you start paying attention to those moments—what excites you, inspires you, or even scares you in the best way—that's when the journey begins.

Maybe you're the visionary. The builder of big, bold ideas. Maybe you're the heart. The one who truly listens, who sees people. Maybe you're the brave one. The one who tries when no one else will.

Whatever your gift is, don't underestimate it. Don't shrink it. Don't wait for permission to use it.

Because the world doesn't need more people just going through the motions. The world needs *you*. Your heart. Your voice. Your gifts. Fully alive. Fully present. Fully unleashed.

Don't hide. Don't hold back. You were created to do something that matters. And every step you take toward what lights you up—no matter how small—is a step toward that purpose.

You matter. Your gifts matter. And the world is waiting for the impact only *you* can make. Are you ready to listen to what your life has been trying to tell you all along? Because the moment you say yes is the moment everything starts to change.

It's not just about the destination. It's about who you're becoming along the way there.

Because the truth is, life isn't a straight line to some final place called "success." It's a journey—a *becoming*. Every step you take, every challenge you face, and every choice you make shape the person you're meant to be.

But let's pause for a moment. Really stop and think about the last time you truly valued who you are right now? Not the version of you you're still working on or the "perfected" version you think the world wants to see, but this version—the one showing up today. The one that's trying, learning, growing, and still moving forward. That version of you? Deserves respect. Deserves love. Deserves to be seen.

Becoming your greatest self isn't about having it all figured out; it's about being honest enough to grow through what you're going through. And that takes courage.

So don't wait until you feel "ready." Don't wait until everything's in place. You are already on the path. And the way you see yourself along the way defines the quality of your journey.

So, ask yourself: Can you honor who you are *right now*—even as you reach for who you're becoming? Because the moment you do, you stop chasing perfection and start walking in purpose. And that's when everything begins to shift.

The way you think about yourself sets the tone for your entire life.

Not your circumstances. Not what others say. You. Your thoughts. Your beliefs.

But let's get real for a second: It's *easy* to fall into the trap of doubt.

It's easy to obsess over everything you haven't done instead of celebrating how far you've come. To scroll through someone else's highlight reel and wonder if you're enough. To let fear whisper lies that your dreams are too big, too bold, too far away.

But here's the truth you need to grab hold of right now: Your thoughts are not your limits. They are your launchpad.

The moment you begin to shift your mindset—from fear to faith, doubt to belief, and judgment to compassion—everything begins to change.

Challenges become growth opportunities. Failure becomes fuel for your future. Comparison loses its grip. All because you start to see the value of your lane, your path, your purpose.

So, ask yourself:

- WHAT STORY ARE YOU TELLING YOURSELF ABOUT WHO YOU ARE?
- ARE YOUR THOUGHTS BUILDING YOU, OR BREAKING YOU?
- ARE YOU MAKING ROOM FOR GROWTH, OR BOXING YOURSELF INTO FEAR?

Your mind is your greatest weapon, or your biggest wall. Nurture it. Challenge it. Protect it. Feed it with truth. Fuel it with vision. And use it to build a life that reflects who you truly are—not who the world expects you to be.

You're powerful. You're worthy. You're capable. And when your mindset matches your potential, there's no limit to what you can become. This journey is yours.

Own it. And choose to think in a way that takes you higher

Who You Are Right Now, You Are Enough

Let's be honest, it's easy to feel like you always have to be *more*. More successful. More confident. More put-together. More everything. But let's stop right here. Take a deep breath.

And let this truth sink in: Who. You. Are. Right. Now. Is. Enough.

Not the "perfect" version of you. Not the future version with all the answers. The you that's here reading this, striving, growing, and showing up.

You're not your past mistakes. You're not your insecurities. You're not your unfinished goals.

You're defined by your courage to keep going, especially on the days that try to break you. Those "hard days"? Those are character-building days. They're proof that you're still in the fight. Still becoming. Still rising.

So, pause for a moment and appreciate this:

- YOU'VE SURVIVED BATTLES OTHERS DON'T EVEN KNOW ABOUT.

- YOU'VE KEPT LEARNING, EVEN WHEN IT FELT UNCOMFORTABLE OR UNCLEAR.

- YOU'VE SHOWN UP—WITH YOUR HEART, YOUR HOPE, AND YOUR HUMANITY—EVEN WHEN IT WAS HARD.

That's strength. That's growth. That's enough. And don't forget: You have something no one else in this world does. Your voice. Your story. Your light.

So, don't waste another second trying to earn your worth. You are already worthy. Worthy of love. Worthy of respect. Worthy of believing in yourself—*now,* not later.

This journey was never about perfection. It's about presence. It's about being you—fully, unapologetically, imperfectly, and boldly. And that is powerful.

Your Future Is Built One Step at a Time

Let's talk about you—the version of you that's becoming.

Maybe you've got big dreams. Maybe you're still figuring it all out. Maybe some days you feel clear, and other days you feel completely lost. That's okay. Becoming the person you're meant to be isn't about some far-off future. It's happening right now. In the choices you make. In the habits you're building. In the way you treat yourself when no one's watching. Every single decision—yes, every one—is shaping your tomorrow.

When you choose to learn, grow, and stretch, you're becoming more capable. When you prioritize your health, peace, and well-being, you're becoming stronger. When you face fear, take the risk, or step into the unknown, you're becoming braver.

Growth doesn't have to be loud. It doesn't have to look impressive on the outside. Sometimes, the most powerful transformation happens quietly, one intentional step at a time. So, stop waiting to become "that" person someday. You are already in the process. You are already becoming.

And even the smallest actions—the ones no one sees—are building a life that reflects your vision, values, and purpose. Keep going. One day. One step. One choice at a time. Because this version of you is already powerful, and where you're headed? That's something worth becoming.

It's Your Journey, Embrace the Process

Here's something we forget way too often: The journey isn't the path to the goal. The journey *is* the goal. It's not just about crossing the finish line or hitting some milestone. It's about who you become on your way there.

It's in the lessons life throws at you when things fall apart. It's in the strength you build when you keep going. It's in the connections, breakthroughs, and quiet moments of joy that show up when you least expect them.

Even the detours are divine. Even the hard days are holy ground. Because they're shaping you—your grit, your grace, your growth. So, if it feels like you're behind, you're not. If it feels like your progress is too small, it's not. Every step counts. Every setback teaches. Every moment is part of your making.

And here's the powerful truth: You don't have to rush. You don't have to have it all figured out. You just have to keep showing up.

Be patient with yourself. Be proud of how far you've come. And keep walking, even when the path feels unclear.

This journey is uniquely yours. It's building something in you that success alone never could. You're not alone. We're all figuring it out.

So, take a deep breath. And trust the journey. It's doing more in you than you know.

Your Life Is Your Legacy

The way you think, the way you grow, and the way you show up matter. More than you know. More than you can see. More than you might believe. When you begin to value how you think, embrace who you are, and lean into who you're becoming, you create a ripple effect that reaches far beyond you.

When you honor your thoughts, you silently give others permission to believe in theirs. When you choose self-acceptance, you create space for others to stop hiding. When you commit to your growth, you light the way for someone else's breakthrough.

Your journey isn't just personal; it's powerful. The way you treat yourself sets the tone for everything. Your family feels it. Your friends feel it. Your community watches it. Even strangers feel your energy long before they hear your words.

Don't underestimate your impact. Don't overlook the quiet shifts you're making. You becoming your best self isn't selfish; it's service. You are part of something bigger. You're living proof that growth is possible, change is real, and becoming isn't about perfection. It's about courage.

So, keep showing up. Keep becoming. Keep choosing to live with intention, because the world is watching. And it's better because of you.

3

Discovering the Real You – Unlock the Power Inside

Have you ever thought about what makes you who you are? Not just your name, hobbies, titles, status, or positions in life, but the real you inside?

Here's something really cool to think about: Your dreams, ideas, and desires are already inside you. They've been there since day one.

Think about this:

The energy of your mom and dad came together to create you, a unique being with a mind, heart, and spirit that can do incredible things. And hidden inside you are seeds, even before you were born. Seeds of greatness. Seeds of your talents, your abilities, your gifts, and your passions, all waiting to grow.

But here's the twist. As you go through life, you're constantly surrounded by people, experiences, and ideas that shape what you think and what you believe.

And guess what? Most of the time, you don't even realize how much your thoughts and beliefs come from outside of you. They can be influenced by family, friends, social media, teachers, even random people you meet.

It's like having a playlist of thoughts that don't necessarily belong to you. It's like finding the right "job" to be, do, and have where you just "fit in."

Now, let's pause and reflect on the word "job" itself. In our society, the word has been largely defined by external expectations: what you do for a living, how you earn money, or what title you hold.

But what if I could redefine "job" to reflect a deeper, more personal journey? One that focuses on your mindset, your character, and how you show up in the world.

The J.O.B. Mindset: Reframing How You Show up in Life

Imagine waking up every day with a sense of excitement, not because you have a "job" to go to, but because you have a journey on which to embark filled with opportunities to grow, connect, and express your unique gifts.

The journey is driven not by the demands of a paycheck but by a purpose, an internal call to live a life that reflects your deepest values and passions. Your day is shaped by the choices you make, not just the tasks you need to complete.

You see, you're not a blank page. The potential to live out your dreams is already inside you. Your life's journey is about discovering those hidden gifts and letting them shine.

All the things you want to achieve—whether it's being successful, happy, or living with purpose—are already in your heart. Your "job" is to uncover them, trust in your unique talents, and believe in your ability to make them real.

So, as you walk through the daily tasks of life and beyond, take a moment to reflect on what you're thinking and believing. Question where those ideas came from and whether they're truly yours.

Your future is not determined by what others say about you. It's determined by what you believe is possible for yourself.

So, instead of a job simply being something you begrudgingly go to for a paycheck, think of a job as a J.O.B. (Journey, Opportunities, Beliefs). This acronym is about the role you take on in all aspects of your life—the Journey you're on, the Opportunities that arise, and the Beliefs that shape your reality.

Journey

Your life is a journey, not a destination. It's about the ongoing process of growth, learning, and self-discovery. Every day is an opportunity to expand your understanding of who you are, what you stand for, and what you can contribute to the world.

The journey isn't always linear, and it's certainly not without challenges, but it's your journey.

How do you approach it? How would you describe seeing each experience, each setback, and each success as part of a larger unfolding narrative? Are you embracing the journey with curiosity and openness, or are you getting caught up in the result?

Opportunities

Opportunities are everywhere. Whether in your career, relationships, or personal growth, life is constantly offering new chances to engage, evolve, create, and contribute. But to recognize and seize these opportunities, you need to have the right mindset.

You must be willing to look beyond the surface, beyond the "status quo," and see what's possible.

This means not just waiting for opportunities to come to you but actively seeking them out—whether it's a new idea, a new connection, or a new way of doing things.

Are you looking at your day with a mindset of possibility, or are you just going through the motions?

Beliefs

Your beliefs are the foundation upon which everything in your life is built. They shape how you think, act, and interact with others. Your beliefs are powerful. They can either limit you or empower you.

What do you believe about yourself, about others, and about the world around you? Do you believe that the world is full of possibilities, or do you see it as a place of competition and scarcity? Do you believe you are worthy of success, love, and happiness, or do you hold limiting beliefs that keep you from living fully?

The Classic Mindset

Now let's consider how the J.O.B. Mindset contrasts with the more common, external view of a "job" in today's world, defined as Judgment, Opinions, and Biases. Let's unpack this side of the coin.

Judgment

Many people approach life with judgment—not just toward others but themselves.

How often do you judge yourself for not being where you think you should be? How often do you judge others based on their actions or choices, without truly understanding their journey?

Judgment closes the door to empathy, compassion, and growth. When you approach life through the lens of judgment, you miss the richness of the human experience, the opportunity to connect deeply and learn from each person you encounter. Instead of judgmental, choose to be curious, open, and understanding.

Opinions

Everyone has opinions. And while it's important to have your own point of view, opinions can often cloud your ability to see the truth. Too many opinions—whether your own or others'—can create noise in your mind, making it harder to connect with your authentic self.

Opinions can make you feel pressured to conform, fit into predefined boxes, or live up to external expectations. But when you base your life on your own ideas instead of the opinions of others, you open yourself up to new possibilities.

How often do you let the opinions of others shape the way you see yourself or the way you navigate your life?

Biases

We all carry biases, whether they're conscious or unconscious, objective or subjective. They're shaped by your past experiences, upbringing, culture, and even society.

Biases can limit our ability to see the full picture, connect with people who are different from us, or embrace new ideas. It often keeps us stuck in old patterns of thinking, preventing growth and transformation.

Can you challenge your biases and approach situations with a fresh set of eyes and an open mind? Can you step outside of your comfort zone and explore perspectives different from your own?

Your J.O.B. Mindset Reflects Your Character

When you start viewing your "job" as a mindset rooted in journey, opportunities, and beliefs, you realize that you're no longer just working through a series of tasks or fulfilling someone else's expectations. You're living out a higher calling, one that invites you to live with purpose, intention, and truth.

This is where character comes into play. Your mindset is directly tied to the strength of your character. The way you approach your journey, how you seize opportunities, and the beliefs you hold about yourself and the world are reflections of who you truly are at your core.

Do you show up as someone who is open-minded, compassionate, and growth-oriented? Or do you let judgment, bias, and limiting beliefs dictate your interactions and your true life's path?

As you engage in your "job"—whether as a business owner, co-worker, friend, spouse, or member of your community—your character shapes how you experience life. It shapes the impact you have on others, the opportunities you attract, and the legacy you leave behind.

The beauty of the J.O.B. Mindset is that it's not confined to a single role. It applies to all aspects of your life. It's not just about what you do; it's about how you do it and why you do it.

When you view life through the lens of journey, opportunities, and beliefs, you take ownership of your experience, you embrace your individuality, and you create a life that reflects the deepest parts of who you are.

You have the power to choose. Your "job", in the truest sense, is about living in alignment with your highest self, showing up with purpose and authenticity, and embracing the journey with all its challenges and possibilities.

When you adopt the J.O.B. Mindset, you unlock the freedom to live your best, most fulfilled life.

What do you think about yourself? What do you believe about your future? And most importantly, where did your thoughts and beliefs even come from?

These questions are important because what you think about yourself today will shape the choices you make tomorrow. Do your beliefs support the amazing person you already are, or do they hold you back?

The more you understand where your thoughts come from, the more power you'll have to create the future you truly want.

Now is the time to start tapping into the seeds of greatness already planted inside you. It's time to become the person you were always meant to be.

4

Unlocking Your Human Potential – The Value of Mindset and Character

What if you knew how much untapped potential is within you? What if you realized that the key to unlocking that potential isn't something outside of you, but something already inside, waiting to be discovered?

Throughout history, the greatest thinkers, educators, motivators, and spiritual leaders have all pointed to this truth: Who you are and what you can achieve are shaped by how you think and the strength of your character.

In my study of personal growth and human potential, I've explored the wisdom of the past and present—drawing on the ideas and teachings of thought leaders who have shaped the way we understand success, fulfillment, and transformation. Their lessons are timeless, yet deeply relevant for the world we live in today.

Here's what they've taught us: The way you think defines the way you live. Your character—the habits, principles, and integrity you develop—determines the legacy you leave behind.

Mindset: The Foundation of Your Growth and Potential

If there's one truth that the greatest minds agree upon, it's that everything begins with your mindset.

A fixed mindset keeps you stuck, believing that your abilities and circumstances are unchangeable. A growth mindset opens doors, teaching you to see challenges as opportunities, failures as lessons, and effort as the path to mastery.

Great thought leaders like Carol Dweck, James Allen, Napoleon Hill, and countless others remind us that our thoughts are not just passing ideas; they're seeds. The thoughts we plant, nurture, and believe will grow into the life we create.

What thoughts are shaping the way you see yourself? Are you approaching life with a mindset of fear and limitation, or courage and possibility? What beliefs are you holding onto that no longer serve you?

Your mindset has the power to reframe every experience, reshape every challenge, and redirect your entire future.

And when you learn to value and master your thinking, you begin to unlock the potential that's been waiting inside you all along.

Character: The Compass That Guides Your Journey

While mindset is the foundation for growth, character is what gives that growth meaning. Who you are—your values, your principles, your standards—is the compass that guides your decisions and shapes the way you live.

The greatest thought leaders remind us: What you achieve matters.

Who you become matters even more.

Success without character is empty, and potential without purpose is unfulfilled.

Developing character means:

- PRACTICING YOUR STANDARDS IS NOT WHAT YOU DO WHEN SOMEONE'S WATCHING; IT'S WHAT YOU DO WHEN NO ONE IS WATCHING.
- LEADING WITH EMPATHY, KINDNESS, AND HUMILITY.
- STAYING DISCIPLINED AND COMMITTED TO YOUR GOALS, EVEN WHEN THE PATH GETS HARD.
- CHOOSING GROWTH OVER COMFORT, HONESTY OVER CONVENIENCE, AND COURAGE OVER FEAR.

As leaders like Viktor Frankl and Stephen Covey have taught us:

- CHARACTER IS BUILT NOT IN THE EASY MOMENTS, BUT IN THE HARD ONES WHEN YOU'RE FACED WITH CHOICES THAT CHALLENGE YOU TO RISE ABOVE YOUR FEARS, EXCUSES, OR DOUBTS.
- IT'S ABOUT ALIGNING WHO YOU ARE WITH WHO YOU WANT TO BECOME.

The Intersection of Thoughts, Mindset, and Character

In studying the ideas of the greatest minds, one thing becomes clear: Personal growth and human potential thrive at the intersection of how you lead your life through your mindset and character.

A strong mindset gives you the belief and tools to grow. A strong character keeps you grounded and aligned with your values as you grow.

Educational pioneers like Maria Montessori and John Dewey have shown us the value of lifelong learning and the importance of thinking critically about the world.

Motivational leaders like Zig Ziglar and Jim Rohn remind us self-discipline and vision are key to creating a life of purpose.

Inspirational voices like Maya Angelou and Brené Brown teach us courage, vulnerability, and resilience are the building blocks of greatness.

Spiritual leaders from Mahatma Gandhi to Thich Nhat Hanh show us true fulfillment comes from living with intention, mindfulness, and compassion.

By drawing on these lessons, you can begin to understand that personal growth isn't just about what you achieve; it's about how you grow into the best versions of yourself for the sake of the people and the world around you.

A Call to Action: Who Are You Becoming?

Here's a question that I believe lies at the heart of personal growth: Who are you becoming along the journey of your life?

It's not just about setting goals or striving for success; it's about who you are in the process. It's about valuing the way you think, treating your mindset like the foundation it is, and building your character as the compass that will guide you toward a meaningful life.

Are you living in alignment with your values? Are you growing in ways that challenge you to stretch beyond your comfort zone? Are you cultivating the mindset and habits that will lead you to become the person you aspire to be?

Personal growth is a lifelong journey; it's not something you "achieve" in a single moment. It is a daily practice, a conscious choice, and a process of becoming.

And when you commit to valuing how you think, who you are, and who you're becoming, you step into the fullest expression of your potential.

PART II:
THE VISION – SEEING BEYOND WHERE YOU ARE

Developing the internal compass to drive purpose and clarity

5

The Vision – Unlocking Your Potential, Inspiring Possibility

In my research and work, my mission is to raise individuals' conscious awareness, inspiring them to unlock their potential by valuing how they think, who they are, and who they are becoming.

By studying the greatest minds of the past and present, I aim to share timeless wisdom that empower you to:

- SHIFT YOUR MINDSET TOWARD GROWTH AND POSSIBILITY.
- BUILD YOUR CHARACTER WITH INTEGRITY AND INTENTION.
- SEE EVERY CHALLENGE AS A STEP TOWARD BECOMING YOUR BEST SELVES.

At the end of the day, your life isn't just about what you do; it's about the legacy you leave through who you were. And the world needs people who are willing to think deeply, grow boldly, and live authentically.

Your Journey Starts Here

If you've ever felt called to do more, grow more, or live with greater purpose, let this be your reminder: The potential is already within you.

The seeds of growth are there, waiting to be nurtured. The person you're becoming is already taking shape, one choice at a time. It starts with how you think. It's guided by who you are. And it leads to who you're becoming.

Keep going. Keep growing. The journey is worth it, and so are you.

The Power of Thought: Unlocking the Potential of Your Mind

It's an uncomfortable truth, but it's one I believe we all need to face: Most people don't truly think.

As George Bernard Shaw so famously put it, "Two percent of people think, three percent of people think they think, and ninety-five percent would rather die than think."

That's a staggering statement. What George Bernard Shaw is alluding to is something we all instinctively know: Many of us go through life on autopilot, reacting to the world around us without ever really pausing to examine how we think, why we think, and what we choose to believe.

We react to situations or follow patterns of thought that have been conditioned into us, but we don't often stop to question:

- IS THIS THE BEST WAY TO THINK?
- IS THIS SERVING MY HIGHEST SELF?

THE VISION

Earl Nightingale, another great thinker, captured this perfectly when he said, "If people said what they were thinking, they'd be speechless."

The sheer volume and randomness of our daily thoughts is overwhelming. According to research, the average person has, at a minimum, sixty thousand thoughts running through their mind on a daily basis. Let that sink in for a moment. Sixty. Thousand.

Most of these thoughts are automatic, habitual, and often negative. The brain is wired to be more reactive than reflective, which means much of what we "think" is just mental noise.

What's even more alarming is that many of these thoughts are on repeat. We think the same thoughts over and over again, often without realizing it.

These thought patterns become so ingrained that they shape our perceptions of ourselves, others, and the world. And sadly, for many of us, those repeated thoughts are not positive or empowering. They're filled with self-doubt, fear, criticism, and limitation.

But here is the good news: You have the power to take control of your thoughts. And that power is where your true potential lies.

If you're not actively thinking, then you're allowing your mind to be shaped by the default programs installed by society, your upbringing, and past experiences.

You let external influences dictate how you feel and what you believe. But when you choose to actively engage with your thoughts, you begin to reclaim your power.

6

The Power of Awareness

The first step in transforming your thought process is awareness. If you don't even recognize that your thoughts are on autopilot, then you're destined to remain stuck in old patterns.

But when you start to pay attention to what's going on in your mind, you can begin to notice how much of it is negativity, limitation, or fear-based thinking. It's amazing how much power comes from simply noticing the stories you tell yourself.

Start by observing your thoughts without judgment. Notice the tone, frequency, and content.

What do you think about yourself? About others? About your life and your future?

If your thoughts are dominated by negativity, it's time to make a shift. The mind, like a muscle, can be retrained. And once you're aware of the patterns, you can choose to change them.

The Mind Is Your Most Powerful Tool

Your thoughts form the foundation of your beliefs, and your beliefs shape your actions. Every action you take, every decision you make, begins with a thought.

The most successful and fulfilled individuals in the world, the ones who truly live their "greatest selves," are incredibly mindful of their thinking. They've learned to direct their minds toward constructive, positive, and empowering thoughts.

If you want to change your life, it starts with changing the way you think. This is not about denying negative thoughts or pretending that you're always happy or positive.

It's about taking ownership of your mental state and making the choice to focus on what's empowering, productive, and aligned with your vision for the future.

Rewire Your Brain

The great thing about the brain is that it has neural plasticity; it can change and adapt in response to experiences.

Through consistent practice, you can replace habitual, negative thoughts with ones that are positive, affirming, and aligned with your true potential. You can train yourself to break free from the repetitive thought patterns that no longer serve you.

One powerful tool in this process is mindfulness, or the practice of staying present and observing your thoughts without getting caught up in them.

When you become more mindful, you create space between the stimulus (the thought or feeling) and your response.

You stop reacting automatically and start choosing how you want to respond. This shift in awareness allows you to redirect your thoughts, even in the midst of negative or challenging situations.

Another tool is affirmations, positive statements that you repeat to yourself, reinforcing a new belief or thought pattern.

They help to reprogram your subconscious mind, replacing old, limiting beliefs with ones that serve your highest good.

The Power of Thought Is Your Greatest Asset

Your thoughts are the gateway to your destiny. The beliefs that you hold, the words that you speak to yourself, and the choices you make all originate in the mind.

If your thoughts are rooted in scarcity, fear, and self-doubt, your actions will follow suit. But if your thoughts are rooted in abundance, possibility, and self-belief, your actions will reflect that.

The mind is not just a tool. It's your greatest asset.

And it's time you start treating it as such. By consciously choosing your thoughts, you align your mind with your highest goals and aspirations. You stop being a passive participant in your life and begin actively shaping your reality

A Call to Action: Transform Your Thoughts, Transform Your Life

It's time to take back control. No more letting your thoughts run wild or hold you back. Start today by becoming aware of your thinking patterns. Observe the thoughts that are on repeat and ask yourself if they're serving your highest good.

Are they empowering you? Are they in alignment with the person you want to become?

If not, begin to challenge them. Replace them with thoughts rooted in possibility, growth, and self-compassion.

Remember, you're the thinker of your thoughts, and the quality of your thoughts determines the quality of your life.

You have the power to think differently. You have the power to think better. And in doing so, you have the power to transform your life. Are you ready to take the first step?

7

Step into the Vision of Your Higher Self

Envision waking up each morning with a fire in your soul and clarity in your heart. No longer just surviving, but rising. Rising with purpose. Rising with peace. Rising with a bold and unshakable knowledge that you are in alignment with your higher self.

This isn't a dream. It's your destiny.

A destiny where every part of you—your talents, gifts, and passions—is not hidden, but fully expressed. Where the actions you take are no longer driven by obligation or fear, but by intention. Where your days are not filled with noise or pressure, but with meaning, joy, and impact.

In this life, you are free. Free to create. Free to grow. Free to give. Free to be everything you were always meant to be.

The abundance that surrounds you isn't just financial; it's emotional, spiritual, and relational. You walk with confidence. You speak with clarity. You live with fulfillment because you're finally tuned in to the truth of who you are.

And that truth? It's powerful. It's radiant. It's real.

But here's what no one tells you: That kind of freedom and alignment doesn't come from following the expectations of the world. It doesn't come from performing for approval, fitting in, or playing small.

It comes from breaking the mold. From getting still enough to hear your own voice. From living in alignment with the values that resonate deep in your soul.

Because when you stop living for everyone else's version of success, you start unlocking your own. You begin to trust the path that's uniquely yours. You step into a rhythm that feels honest, whole, and undeniably YOU.

The life you've imagined isn't far away. It's here, waiting for you to claim it.

So, take this moment. Exhale the pressure. Silence the noise. Look inward. And ask yourself:

"What does my greatest life—my truest self—really look like?"

Then commit to attracting that with everything you've got.

Because the world doesn't need another copy. It needs YOU—fully alive, fully aligned, and finally free.

Six Key Foundational Areas

Before your dreams take flight, your life must be grounded on something solid. These six foundational areas are the pillars upon which your purpose, peace, and power are built. Each one is connected. Each one must be nurtured. Together, they unlock the greatest version of you.

Take a moment to reflect on the foundation of your life. And as you live out your daily life, think about these key areas. Ask yourself:

- AM I DEVELOPING THIS AREA OF MY LIFE?
- AM I INTENTIONAL ABOUT HOW I SHOW UP HERE?
- WHERE CAN I GROW?

Self-Image: The Foundation of Who You Are

The first area is self-image. It's the foundation of everything you think, say, and do. It shapes the way you navigate the world, the decisions you make, and the opportunities you attract. Your life will only grow to the level of the vision you hold for yourself.

What is the image you want and desire for your life? How do you currently see yourself?

Personal Relationships: Intimately and Socially

The quality of your relationships often mirrors the quality of your relationship with yourself.

Your relationships are reflections—of your confidence, your boundaries, your love, your energy. How you speak to yourself determines how you speak to others. What you believe you deserve sets the standard for the love and respect you allow in.

What are you saying to yourself about who you are and what you deserve? How do you show up in your relationships with others and with yourself?

Mental Wellbeing: Guard Your Mind

Your emotional state, your focus, your peace of mind—it's all shaped by what you feed your mind.

What you read, listen to, watch, and think about daily is either building you up or breaking you down. You are the gatekeeper. You must protect your thoughts like your future depends on it, because it does.

What are you feeding your mind? What are you listening to, reading, and watching?

Fill your mind with peace, power, and purpose.

Physical Health: The Temple of Your Being

Your body is not just a vessel; it's a sacred tool for your pursuit in life.

Without health, freedom fades. Without energy, dreams dim. Without vitality, vision is hard to attract. When you honor your body, you strengthen your mind, spirit, and life's momentum.

How are you treating your body? Are you giving it the rest, nutrition, and movement it deserves?

When you care for your body, it responds by fueling your greatness.

Personal Growth and Development: Where Are You Investing Your Time?

Your time is your most valuable asset. It tells the truth about what you value.

Growth is not something you stumble into. It's a choice. It's intentional. It's the seed of every next-level version of you. The only way to become who you were meant to be is by constantly investing in your own growth.

Are you wasting time or working your time? How are you feeding your potential?

Time will never run out, but your life will. So, put more life in your time.

Personal Finances: The Energy of Your Money

Money is not your identity. It's a tool, not a measure of your worth. It flows where it's invited and stays where it's welcomed and respected.

Your relationship with money reflects your values, habits, and mindset. Wealth isn't about how much you have, but about how wisely you manage what you've been given. When you master your money, you expand your freedom and impact.

What do you believe about money? How are you managing it? Are you letting it control you, or are you in control of it?

Money is not your worth; it's your resource. Use it with purpose.

Bringing It All Together: A Life in Alignment Is a Life in Power

Each of these six areas is a thread in the fabric of your life.

When one is weak, the whole pattern suffers. But when you intentionally strengthen each one, you unlock alignment, clarity, and unstoppable momentum.

What does the best version of you look like in each area? Where can you begin today? How can you use these foundations to transform not just your life, but the lives of those around you?

You were created for more. Now is the time to build the life that reflects it. When you commit to living in alignment with these values, you create a ripple effect that impacts not just your life but your community and the world around you.

8

The Chase for "Living the Dream"

We all know it. The familiar, almost universal phrase "Living the Dream." It's something we hear or see on all sides—from family, friends, colleagues, and acquaintances to social media posts, titles on magazine covers, and songs on the radio.

At first glance, it seems like a phrase packed with promise, with the lure of fulfillment, success, and happiness. But when we take a step back and really think about it:

- WHAT DOES "LIVING THE DREAM" REALLY MEAN?
- AND, MORE IMPORTANTLY, WHOSE DREAM IS IT?

In conversations, advertisements, and the flashing images throughout our daily lives, how often is the dream tied to visible symbols of success—money, prestigious titles, and social status?

We're conditioned to believe that these are the ultimate markers of a life well-lived, the outward signs that we've "made it." After all, if you've reached the top, achieved financial freedom, or attained that coveted position or title, surely you must be living the dream, right?

But here are the deeper questions:

- IS THAT REALLY THE DREAM YOU SHOULD BE CHASING?
- IS IT POSSIBLE THAT IN THIS ENDLESS PURSUIT OF EXTERNAL VALIDATION, YOU RISK LOSING SIGHT OF THE MORE FUNDAMENTAL QUALITIES THAT MAKE YOU WHO YOU TRULY ARE?

The qualities that define you do so not by what you have, but who you are. Qualities like integrity, empathy, authenticity, and self-awareness. Qualities that no amount of money, job title, or social media follower count can truly measure.

Perhaps the goals you set for yourself—those markers of success—aren't inherently wrong. In fact, they can be valuable reflections of your ambition, drive, and personal growth.

However, when the pursuit of these external symbols becomes the sole definition of success, you may inadvertently dilute the very essence of your character.

The chase for recognition, power, and wealth can sometimes mask the very things that make you feel whole, content, and at peace with who you are.

THE CHASE FOR "LIVING THE DREAM"

Let's explore this tension between the external "dream" and the internal call to be the greatest version of yourself.

Let's dive into how the pursuit of external success can sometimes cloud your deeper purpose, and how you can learn to live a life that reflects your truest values.

What if living the dream isn't about what you have or where you stand, but about who you become during the process?

What if the greatest success lies in creating the life that feels truly authentic to you?

What if this life doesn't just fit someone else's definition of success, but matches your own?

Let's take a moment to step away from the noise. To reflect on what truly matters—not just on the outside, but on the inside. Let's examine the real essence of your being.

Are you ready to go on this journey, to explore the principles of your mindset and character? The dream may be closer than you think.

PART III: THE TRANSFORMATION – ALIGNING WHO YOU ARE WITH WHO YOU'RE BECOMING

Building identity, resilience, and a life aligned with values

9

Unlocking Your Greatest You

As I reflected on my own journey, the ups and downs, the moments of successes and failures, one thing became abundantly clear: The path to becoming your greatest you is never found in the pursuit of external symbols of success—money, titles, or status.

True fulfillment comes when you look inward, align your actions with your core values, and tap into universal truths. These truths have guided some of the most impactful thinkers and leaders in history.

This realization led me to create a framework for living that doesn't just appear successful but is successful in the truest sense. I call it the i.C.A.A.R.E. Mindset.

It stands for six simple, yet powerful principles designed to strengthen your character and empower you to live as the best version of yourself.

When you embody these principles, you don't just exist—you thrive. You become aligned with something much greater than the temporary goals or superficial aspirations that society often pushes on you.

Here are the principles:

i – Individuality

C – Communication

A – Awareness

A – Accountability

R – Responsibility

E – Expectations

By focusing on these core qualities, you'll begin to live a life that aligns with who you truly are, not who others expect you to be.

Examine your own life, your values, your beliefs, and your decisions. Identify where you've been living in alignment with the i.C.A.A.R.E. Mindset and where you perhaps have been pulled off course.

You may have been chasing the dream that everyone else was chasing, but now it's time to ask yourself:

- WHAT IS MY DREAM?
- WHAT DOES MY GREATEST SELF LOOK LIKE?
- HOW DO I BEGIN TO WALK THAT PATH TO START ATTRACTING THE LIFE I DESIRE TODAY?

You hold the power to build a life that's in line with your true self—one that amplifies your character, deepens your purpose, and leads to true fulfillment. This is your journey, your opportunity to step into the fullness of who you are.

By incorporating these universal principles into your life, you'll raise your level of awareness, deepen your self-understanding, and align your actions with your highest values.

This mindset empowers you to define your own true-life path. It enables you to make choices that reflect your core values, allowing you to live not only your dream, but a dream that is authentic, purposeful, and deeply meaningful.

This mindset helps you move beyond societal pressures and external definitions of success, inviting you to build a life that truly reflects the greatness within you.

As you begin to apply these principles, you'll find that your mindset shifts. You'll feel more in control, more aligned with your purpose, and more inspired to create a life that resonates with your truest self.

The path to becoming your greatest you requires continuous self-awareness, growth, and action. But with the i.C.A.A.R.E. Mindset, you'll have the tools, principles, clarity, and the foundation to live a life that's meaningful, impactful, and uniquely yours.

The journey starts now, and with each principle you apply, you're moving closer to the greatest version of yourself.

The power to change is in your hands. Will you choose to unlock it?

10

The Principle of Individuality – Living Your Truest Expression

What if tomorrow didn't just feel like another day, but a calling? What if the moment your eyes opened, you felt lit up from the inside—driven not by duty, but Individuality?

Imagine waking up not to the noise of expectation, but to the rhythm of your own purpose. Not rushing to meet the world's standards, but rising to live your truth—with joy, boldness, and intention. This isn't a dream. This is possible. This is power. This is purpose.

You were never meant to shrink yourself to fit in. You were meant to stand out and shine. You were created to live fully, love deeply, and lead from a place of truth. Your passions aren't random. Your talents weren't a mistake. Your voice wasn't meant to stay silent. You are here to move something in this world.

So, what would it feel like to know that everything you do, everything you are, is making a real impact? What would it feel like to wake up knowing you're in the right place, doing the right thing, and being the real you?

It would feel like freedom, abundance, fulfillment. It would fill you with an unshakable sense of joy that can't be taken away because it wasn't given by others—it was born within you.

When you align with your individuality and stop apologizing for who you are and start living from the inside out, you become unbreakable.

You stop chasing validation and start creating vibration—the kind that moves people, the kind that opens doors, the kind that says: "I know who I am, and I'm here to live it out loud."

And from that place, abundance flows. Not just money, but meaning. Not just success, but significance. You begin to live a life where everything makes sense because it all aligns. So, let this be your reminder: You don't need permission. You don't need to wait. You don't need to be perfect. You just need to be you. Boldly. Bravely. Unapologetically.

The world doesn't need another copy. It needs you in full color, truth, and purpose. This is your moment to rise. To align. To become. Not someday. Not one day. But today.

11

The Principle of Communication – How You Show Up Speaks Volumes

Communication is far more than just the words we speak. It's the heartbeat of human connection, the bridge between hearts and minds, and the tool through which we express ourselves and understand each other.

Yet, when we think about communication, most of us focus solely on what we say. But here's the truth: Words make up only a small portion of the message you're conveying.

In fact, research reveals:

- ONLY 7 PERCENT OF COMMUNICATION COMES FROM THE WORDS THEMSELVES.

- A STAGGERING 38 PERCENT COMES FROM HOW YOU SAY THOSE WORDS: THE TONE, RHYTHM, AND THE INFLECTION IN YOUR VOICE.

- THE OTHER 55 PERCENT IS YOUR BODY LANGUAGE, THE UNSPOKEN SIGNALS THAT REVEAL MORE ABOUT YOUR TRUE THOUGHTS AND FEELINGS THAN ANY WORD COULD EVER CAPTURE.

That means that vast majority of the power of communication, 93 percent, is non-verbal. Every time you communicate, you're transmitting a wealth of information not just through your words, but through how you stand, the look on your face, the gestures you make, the tones to your words, and even the energy you project.

Have you ever felt the truth behind someone's words before they even finished speaking?

Maybe their tone was polite, but something just didn't feel right. Their words said one thing, but their body said something else. Arms crossed. Eyes avoiding yours. A forced smile that didn't reach their heart.

You sensed it. You felt it. Because communication isn't just about what's said; it's about what's shown.

Now, flip the script. Remember a time when someone didn't say much, but their energy, tone, and presence made you feel truly seen. No grand speech. No perfect phrasing. Just a nod, a warm glance, and a posture that said, "I'm here with you."

That is the power of non-verbal connection. That's what happens when words and energy align—when authenticity speaks louder than sound.

It's not just about what you say. It's about how you show up. Because people may forget your exact words, but they'll never forget how your presence made them feel.

So, ask yourself:

- ARE YOU JUST SPEAKING, OR ARE YOU CONNECTING?
- ARE YOUR WORDS MATCHING YOUR PRESENCE, OR ARE THEY HIDING YOUR TRUTH?
- ARE YOU SHOWING UP IN A WAY THAT INVITES TRUST, EMPATHY, AND REAL IMPACT?

This is your moment to align your communication with your heart, to be intentional with your message and your energy. Because when you master the unspoken, you begin to influence in ways words alone never could.

And the world? It's craving that kind of connection. Keep reading because this is where real influence begins.

How You Show Up Matters More Than You Think

Every time you interact with someone, you're communicating far beyond the words you choose. How you show up—physically, emotionally, and energetically—creates an environment of connection and trust.

Whether you're talking to a colleague, a friend, a spouse, or leading a team, the way you communicate influences how others perceive you, trust you, and engage with you. You're continuously transmitting messages, whether you're aware of it or not.

Build Rapport Through Effective Communication

Want to build real, lasting relationships—personally, professionally, and in everyday life? It starts with one powerful skill: presence.

It's not just about what you say. It's about how you show up. Your body speaks volumes before your words ever do. And when your presence and message align, you unlock something rare—trust.

Trust is the heartbeat of connection. It's the invisible thread that makes people lean in, open up, and feel safe.

The moment you learn to align your tone, body language, and words, you step into a new level of influence and authenticity.

Actively Listen

You don't build connection by waiting for your turn to talk. You build it by listening with your whole self. Nod. Make eye contact. Lean in. Put the phone down. When people feel heard, they feel valued, and that's where bonds begin.

Be Present

Presence is power. You can't fake it. You can't multitask it. It's felt in the energy of the moment. When you truly show up—without distractions—you communicate: *"You matter to me."*

Align Words and Actions

If your words say "I care," but your posture says, "I'm closed," guess what people will believe? Your actions. Your tone. Your energy.

Real connection happens when your message is embodied, when every part of you is saying the same thing.

Have Empathy and Respect

Connection thrives in understanding. Mirroring someone's pace, posture, or energy says, "I'm with you." It doesn't have to be exact; it just has to be genuine.

Read the Room

What's not being said matters just as much as what is. Pay attention to their cues: Are they open? Shut down? Excited? Guarded? Connection deepens when you listen not just with your ears, but with your awareness.

This is how leaders are born and relationships are strengthened.

This is how impact is made, not by just saying the right words, but by becoming the message.

So, ask yourself:

- ARE YOU TRULY PRESENT WHEN IT MATTERS MOST?
- DO YOUR WORDS MATCH YOUR ENERGY?
- ARE YOU BUILDING RAPPORT THAT LEADS TO REAL TRUST, OR JUST SURFACE-LEVEL EXCHANGE?

The people around you can feel the difference. And when you lead with alignment—when your words, tone, and presence move in unison— you don't just speak to minds; you speak to hearts.

Your Unspoken Truth

Words are important. They're the tools you use to share your ideas, thoughts, and emotions. But it's the unspoken that often speaks louder than words themselves.

Your body language, tone, and the way you show up in a conversation tell a story all their own. When you become aware of this, you unlock a whole new dimension of communication that allows you to connect with others on a much deeper level.

By aligning your words, tone, and body language, you build trust, empathy, and understanding. You model the kind of communication that not only creates rapport but also fosters meaningful relationships.

When you communicate with truthfulness, intention, and awareness, you set the stage for stronger connections, deeper trust, and more fulfilling interactions.

The next time you step into a conversation, remember that you're not just speaking; you're expressing, connecting, and building bridges with every gesture, tone, and glance. Your body and your voice speak the truth of who you are, and that truth is what others will resonate with the most.

Communication is the foundational life skill of all great relationships. It's how you connect with others, build trust, and form meaningful bonds. Being able to express yourself clearly and listen with empathy will set you apart.

12

The Principle of Awareness – The Heart of Unlocking Your Greatest You

Awareness is the cornerstone of all the other principles. This is not just about being aware of what you think or do on the surface—it's about understanding the depths of your inner self.

It's about recognizing your thoughts, emotions, behaviors, and the motivations behind them, and then consciously choosing to align them with your highest values and your deepest truth.

It's the guiding force that shapes your perspective and drives your decisions, interactions, and personal growth. It's the foundation that enables you to live an empowered, purposeful life.

Awareness goes beyond simply knowing who you are. It's about how you live, how you engage with the world around you, and how you respond to the internal and external stimuli that life throws your way.

The more aware you are of your thoughts, emotions, and actions, the more intentional you become in shaping your reality.

The more you consciously see yourself, the more power you have to choose your path, your response, and your outcomes.

The Key Skills of Awareness

At its core, awareness isn't a passive state of being. It requires active engagement with your inner being and the willingness to be honest and vulnerable with yourself.

To understand yourself, you need to tap into four essential skills: Empathy, Compassion, Courage, and Curiosity.

Empathy

Empathy begins with understanding yourself. Before you can understand others, you must first recognize your own emotions and thoughts without judgment. It means taking a step back to listen to your inner voice, your desires, and your struggles.

It's the ability to recognize and understand your emotions and the emotions of others. When you can empathize with yourself—when you are aware of your feelings, your triggers, and your responses—you're better able to empathize with others, creating deeper connections and more meaningful relationships.

Empathy allows you to feel and relate to another person's perspective without judgment. It helps you see the world not just from your vantage point, but from theirs.

It's the foundation of true connection and understanding, and it begins with a conscious, internal process of tuning in to yourself.

Compassion

Where empathy allows you to understand, compassion is what moves you to action.

Compassion is the ability to feel for someone in their pain or struggle and to want to help alleviate it, including your own.

It starts with self-compassion: being gentle with yourself when you fall short, understanding that mistakes are a natural part of growth, and offering yourself grace when needed.

When you're self-aware, you recognize the moments you're being too hard on yourself, or when you're shutting down your own needs. Compassion for yourself allows you to forgive and heal, which then expands outward.

The more compassionate you are toward yourself, the more genuine and unconditional compassion you can offer to others. It becomes a ripple effect of kindness and care that improves relationships and creates a nurturing environment, inside and out.

Courage

Awareness isn't always comfortable. In fact, the journey of self-discovery often brings up truths you might rather not confront. But courage enables you to face these truths head-on, without running away or ignoring them.

Courage is not the absence of fear, but the willingness to act despite it. It's the strength to look inward and acknowledge the things you've avoided, the patterns you've fallen into, or the fears you've held onto.

With courage, you begin to face your challenges with a mindset of growth, viewing obstacles as opportunities to evolve.

It allows you to confront your discomfort, your shadow, and your limitations, and use those very things as encouragement for transformation.

The more courageous you are in your awareness, the more empowered you become to shape your life in a way that aligns with your highest truth.

Curiosity

Curiosity is the stimulus for continuous learning and growth. To be self-aware means to approach your life with the attitude of a student, always open to learning more about yourself, your beliefs, your behaviors, and how you can improve.

When you cultivate curiosity, you're not fixed in your ways; you're constantly evolving.

Curiosity allows you to ask the tough questions:

- WHY DID I RESPOND THAT WAY?
- WHAT WAS REALLY BEHIND THAT EMOTION?
- HOW CAN I APPROACH THIS SITUATION DIFFERENTLY?

It's an attitude of exploration, an openness to new perspectives and new experiences, and the desire to improve.

Curiosity makes awareness a dynamic, ongoing process. It helps you understand yourself more deeply and approach challenges with an open mind, making room for growth and transformation.

With empathy, compassion, courage, and curiosity, you become the architect of your own transformation.

These skills, along with the following six higher intellectual faculties and seven universal laws, connect to empower your mindset and character.

Six Higher Intellectual Faculties

Welcome to the world of your inner potential—the realm where your mind holds the power to shape the life you truly aspire to.

The six key principles of your higher intellectual faculties—Will, Reason, Memory, Imagination, Intuition, and Perception—form the foundation of your SuperPowers.

These intellectual faculties not only guide the way you think, but they're also the driving forces behind how you manifest your dreams, ideas, and deepest desires.

Each of these powers plays a unique role in empowering you to engage consciously with your aspirations. They're the tools that allow you to tap into your highest potential and transform your intentions into tangible results.

By deepening your understanding of these principles, you unlock a more profound influence over your thoughts and actions, fueling your journey toward motivation, inspiration, and lasting impact.

You'll learn how to harness and activate them, enabling you to think in a way that propels you forward with purpose and confidence.

Get ready to dive deep into the powerful landscape of your own mind because the life you want begins with how you choose to engage with your SuperPowers.

The SuperPowers of Your Mind

To successfully reprogram your mindset, you must use your six intellectual faculties—your mind's SuperPowers—to consciously shape your thoughts and direct your energy.

By harnessing these powers, you can intentionally shift your paradigm and align your actions with the life you want to create.

Will

Will is the strength to persist in the face of challenges and distractions. It's your ability to stay focused on your new beliefs, even when old paradigms try to creep back in.

Reason

Reason allows you to accept and reject any thoughts that enter your mind and evaluate your beliefs and ideas. Use this faculty to critically assess your paradigm and determine if it's serving you or limiting you. Challenge your old beliefs and replace them with empowering ones.

Memory

Your memory is your power of recall, a tool for reinforcing your new paradigm. By recalling past successes and the moments when you've overcome challenges, you can build confidence and reinforce new beliefs.

Imagination

You implement your imagination, the fourth dimension of power, to envision the person you want to become, the life you want to live, and the goals you want to achieve. It creates the mental images that direct your thoughts and actions.

Intuition

The inner nudge and voice. Trust your intuition to guide you toward the right decisions. Your inner wisdom can help you navigate the changes necessary to shift your paradigm and follow the path that aligns with your highest self.

Perception

As Dr. Wayne Dyer profoundly states, "When you change the way you look at things, the things you look at change."

You can choose how you perceive your circumstances. Instead of seeing setbacks as failures, choose to see them as opportunities for growth. Change your perspective, and your reality will shift.

The Seven Universal Laws and Your Mindset Mastery

In the pursuit of personal growth and living your best life, understanding the deeper strengths that regulate our reality can be an incredible game-changer. Your mindset—the lens through which you view the world—determines the quality of your experiences, your actions, and your outcomes.

However, as you grow in awareness, you realize that there is an invisible energy, a set of universal laws, which work in alignment with your thoughts and actions to reveal aspects of your life.

These laws are not just ideal concepts; they're powerful principles that govern the very nature of reality and your place within it.

When you consciously align your thoughts and actions with these laws, you unlock your true potential. This is where the magic happens.

The following seven universal laws provide a profound understanding of the natural order of the universe. They are the design for how things work. When you can harness the energy of these principles with your six intellectual faculties, you can elevate your conscious and subconscious mindsets to achieve extraordinary results.

The Seven Universal Laws

Law of Polarity

The law of polarity teaches us that every action has an equal and opposite reaction. Everything in life exists in polarity: light and dark, hot and cold, success and failure. It's easy to view challenges as setbacks, but this law reminds us that failure is essential for growth. Without distinction, there would be no definition or appreciation for the good things in life.

Your thoughts and actions are the seeds for what you'll experience. The key is to embrace the full spectrum of experience. Understand that every negative situation or setback can be reflected by a positive outcome. And when things seem to be at their worst, it's often because you're on the verge of something great. The law of polarity teaches you to shift your focus and perspective.

Using will, you can consciously choose to focus on the positive aspects of any situation, transforming challenges into opportunities. Your ability to rationalize and find solutions, no matter how difficult the situation, activates the law of polarity to work in your favor.

Law of Vibration

Everything in the universe is in a constant state of motion, vibrating at a certain frequency. This includes your thoughts, feelings, and beliefs. The energy you emit through your thoughts and emotions attracts similar energy, often referred to as the law of attraction.

If you desire success, joy, and abundance, your thoughts must align with these frequencies. To raise your vibration, you must consciously focus on positive, empowering thoughts and emotions. Your vibrational energy becomes your magnetic field, drawing people, situations, and opportunities that align with that energy.

Through the power of imagination, one of your SuperPowers, you can vividly visualize yourself living in alignment with the vibrations of what you desire. Imagine the feeling of experiencing your dreams. This activates the law of vibration, attracting the conditions and circumstances necessary for you to bring your vision to life.

Law of Gender

The law of gender reminds us that every creation requires time, care, and development to bring it into physical form. Just as a seed needs time, soil, and water to grow into its creation, your ideas, dreams, and goals require incubation and gestation. This law teaches us the importance of patience and persistence.

In the context of your mindset, the law of gender underscores the importance of nurturing your goals with intention, clarity, and action. Just like a garden, you must tend to your dreams consistently, taking inspired action every day, even when you don't see immediate results.

Trust that with the right care and attention, the seed of your vision will eventually develop.

Law of Cause and Effect

Every effect has a specific cause. Your thoughts, feelings, and actions are the causes, and the results you experience are the effects.

This law emphasizes that you are the creator of your reality, and your consistent thoughts and behaviors will lead to the circumstances you encounter in life.

Using your intuition, the ability to instinctively know what's right for you, helps one understand the cause-and-effect relationship.

When you trust your intuition, you're able to align your actions with your highest good. It guides you toward choices that align with your higher self.

With your conscious awareness, you can choose thoughts, words, and actions that align with the effect you desire.

Instead of reacting mindlessly, take charge of your life by making intentional choices that lead to the outcomes you truly want.

Law of Rhythm

The law of rhythm reminds us that everything in life follows in a natural cycle or rhythm. The seasons change, the tides ebb and flow, and even our energy levels fluctuate throughout the day. Life has a rhythm, and so do you. Every area of your life has a natural flow, and the key is to be in sync with it.

By understanding your own rhythm, you can optimize your mental and emotional cycles. Recognize when you're in a high-energy phase and when you need rest and renewal.

Aligning with this rhythm helps you flow more gracefully through your life, avoiding unnecessary resistance.

You can utilize your memory to reflect on past experiences and recognize patterns in your life. By doing so, you can understand your own rhythms and adjust your actions to be in harmony with your natural flow. This alignment creates less stress and more effortless success.

Law of Relativity

According to the law of relativity, everything in life is relative. No situation is completely good or bad; it's always relative to something else. You can transform any challenge by putting it into context and understanding its position relative to other aspects of your life.

Using your reasoning, you can begin viewing challenges as opportunities to gain experience and transcend the limitations of your circumstances.

When you shift your perspective and apply your intellectual faculties to transform adversity into growth, you elevate your situation to a higher state of energy and success.

Law of Perpetual Transmutation

This is the law of energy transformation. It also relates to the idea of transmutation, the constant conversion of energy into physical form. It asserts that energy is constantly in motion and always in the process of being transmuted from one form to another.

When you direct your thoughts and intentions toward a specific goal, you're transmuting mental energy into physical results.

Every thought you hold has the potential to create an energetic shift in your environment. Using your will, you can focus your thoughts and energy on positive outcomes, gradually transmuting your desires into physical realities.

The law of perpetual transmutation tells us that nothing remains stagnant; you can transform your world simply by changing the energy you bring to it.

Empowering Your Mindset with the Universal Laws

By integrating these seven universal laws into your mindset and character, you unlock a transformative process in your life.

The laws are not just theoretical concepts; they are practical principles that can be applied daily to guide your thoughts, actions, and interactions.

Your SuperPowers, the six intellectual faculties, serve as the tools that amplify these laws. Together, they empower you to shift your energy, raise your vibration, focus your thoughts, and transform your life.

By consciously applying these laws and faculties, you elevate your mindset to a place where you're no longer a passive observer of life, but an active creator of your reality.

As you move forward, remember that the thoughts you think, the emotions you feel, and the actions you take will all align with the natural laws of the universe.

When you align your inner world with these universal principles, you tap into a boundless source of power to create, grow, and live your greatest life.

Unlocking the Power Within: Reprogramming Your Paradigm for Greater Success

At the core of who you are lies a hidden influence that shapes your every thought, feeling, and action. This influence is your paradigm—a mental program, deeply ingrained within your subconscious, that controls almost all of your habitual behaviors. It's the lens through which you view the world and interpret reality.

As Bob Proctor so eloquently puts it, "A paradigm is a mental program that has almost exclusive control over our habitual behaviors, and almost all of our behaviors are habitual."

Your paradigm doesn't just influence small, inconsequential habits; it shapes your life's path. It controls your responses, dictates your comfort zone, and ultimately determines your results. As one consultant wisely stated, "Our results are a direct reflection of what our paradigm is showing us."

What you see externally is a mirror of what's happening internally. Your paradigm is the design of your subconscious mind, filled with beliefs, values, and habits formed over a lifetime.

So, as you look at your life, the question is: What is your paradigm showing you?

The Power of Habit: Shaping Your Subconscious Mind

At an early age, you were unknowingly programmed by your environment—your parents, teachers, friends, and society. These influences shaped your beliefs and behaviors, often without you being consciously aware of it.

You learned to respond based on the mental scripts you absorbed, creating patterns that became your habitual way of thinking, feeling, and acting. Many of these mental scripts are caught not taught.

Dr. Wayne Dyer, one of the greatest thought leaders of our time, uses a profound metaphor to illustrate how our paradigms work.

He asks us to imagine an orange. When you squeeze an orange, you can only get orange juice. No matter how hard you squeeze it, no matter how you try, the juice inside will always be orange.

Comparably, when life squeezes you—when challenges arise, when you're under pressure—the only thing that can come out of you is what's inside.

So, what's inside of you? Are your habitual thoughts, emotions, and beliefs empowering or limiting you? When life challenges you, do you respond with fear, anger, or doubt? Or do you respond with calm, positivity, and resilience?

The Snake Bite: The Silent Poison of Your Negative Thoughts

Dr. Wayne Dyer also speaks of the analogy of a snake bite. He says, "You never die from the snake bite. It's the venom that goes to and through your body that slowly kills you."

In the same way, negative thoughts and beliefs are like venom to your well-being. A single thought doesn't kill you, but the accumulation of toxic, limiting beliefs over time can slowly poison your spirit, your relationships, and your success.

When you hold onto fear, doubt, anger, or resentment, you're letting venom flow through your mind and body.

Negative thoughts and emotions accumulate in your subconscious, building a toxic paradigm that dictates your behavior and sabotages your success.

It's not the occasional negative thought that does the damage. It's the repetition, the habitual thinking, and the deep-rooted beliefs that carry the venom and continue to affect every part of your life.

This is why it's so important to take control of your paradigm and replace old, limiting beliefs with empowering ones.

Buckminster Fuller famously said, "You never change things by fighting the existing reality. To change something, build a new model that makes the existing model obsolete."

Every thought you think shapes your paradigm, and your paradigm controls your results. If you want to change your life, you must change your paradigm.

Reprogramming Your Paradigm: A Shift in Your Thinking

Your paradigm directly impacts your life in every way, so how can you ensure it's healthy?

The answer lies in the power of conscious thinking.

First, recognize that your paradigm is not fixed. Just like the programs on a computer, paradigms can be reprogrammed. You're not a prisoner of your past experiences or your current circumstances.

The power to change your paradigm lies in your ability to shift your thoughts and reprogram your subconscious mind.

Bob Proctor emphasizes that paradigms are simply habits of thought that can be changed with new, empowering beliefs. The key is repetition. The more you practice positive, empowering thoughts, the more they will overwrite the old, limiting beliefs. It's like installing new software on your computer.

When you consistently feed your mind with the right thoughts—thoughts of abundance, success, peace, and joy—you're reprogramming your subconscious mind and changing your paradigm.

The Path to Reprogramming: Your Call to Action

To begin reprogramming your paradigm, you must first identify your current beliefs.

What thoughts, habits, or patterns are you holding onto that no longer serve you? Are you holding onto fear, guilt, or doubt?

If so, it's time to let go. Start by consciously challenging your old beliefs. Ask yourself:

- ARE THESE BELIEFS TRUE?
- ARE THEY EMPOWERING?
- ARE THEY LEADING TOWARD MY DESIRED OUTCOME, OR ARE THEY HOLDING ME BACK?

Then, use the power of affirmations, visualization, and positive thinking to reprogram your subconscious mind. Create new, empowering beliefs that align with your vision of the person you want to become and the life you want to live.

Remember, you're the creator of your reality. The thoughts you think today are shaping your tomorrow. If you want a different result, change your thinking. If you want to experience a different life, change your paradigm. The power lies within you.

As you take control of your paradigm and begin to shift your habitual thoughts and beliefs, you'll begin to see new results—results aligned with your true potential. So, don't wait for life to squeeze you.

Choose what comes out of you. Choose thoughts that empower you. Feelings that uplift you. Actions that propel you forward.

Your results will follow. But it starts with how you see yourself.

Your Mirror Image: The Reflection of Who You're Becoming

Have you ever paused to consider the people you spend the most time with and what they reflect about you? It's a thought-provoking question, one that can offer profound insight into your personal growth and the life you're creating.

Jim Rohn once said, "You're the average of the five people you spend the most time with."

This statement holds a deeper truth than you often realize. It speaks to the energy, qualities, and behaviors that you unconsciously adopt through your closest relationships.

Think about someone who greatly influences your life. Perhaps it's a family member, a close friend, a mentor, or someone you deeply admire. These individuals shape your perspective in ways that can be both empowering and challenging.

What do you love and value about them? What characteristics do you admire, even desire to express?

If you look closely, you'll find that many of these qualities are not only those you appreciate in others, but they're likely reflections of what you love and value about yourself—or what you'd like to grow and evolve in yourself.

When you spend time with someone who exudes kindness, generosity, and compassion, these are qualities that likely resonate with you on some level because you possess them or desire to develop them.

It's the same when you admire someone's work ethic, sense of humor, or intelligence. These traits you value are not by accident; they reflect your own aspirations, ideals, and values. They are mirrored in the people around you because, at a deep level, you recognize and resonate with them.

But here's the twist to your mirror image that often goes unnoticed: The opposite is equally true.

What you dislike or find challenging in others often reflects something within yourself. *If you spot it, you got it.*

This may sound uncomfortable at first, but let's unpack it. Think about the traits that irritate you in others—maybe it's someone's arrogance, their lack of empathy, or perhaps a behavior that rubs you the wrong way.

The truth is, those traits often trigger something inside you, because they're qualities you either don't like to express in yourself or haven't fully acknowledged yet. They may be aspects of your own characteristics or past behaviors you wish to avoid or suppress.

When we're triggered by someone's behavior, it's often a reflection of unresolved feelings or parts of yourself you haven't fully integrated.

Perhaps there's a little bit of that arrogance within you that you've denied, or a lack of patience you're unwilling to confront.

The energy we react to in others is often the energy we carry within ourselves—whether consciously or subconsciously.

Your Mirror Is Always Reflecting

This means you have the power to transform not only the way you relate to others, but also the way you relate to yourself.

The people around you are mirrors, reflecting the qualities you possess, positive and negative. They are like a life-sized, emotional mirror that shows you what's going on inside your own heart and mind.

When you find yourself in a situation where you feel triggered by someone else's behavior, instead of pointing fingers or criticizing them, begin by asking:

- WHAT'S THIS REACTION TELLING ME ABOUT MYSELF?
- COULD THIS BE AN OPPORTUNITY TO UNCOVER SOMETHING ABOUT MY ATTITUDES, BEHAVIORS, OR BELIEFS I HAVEN'T FULLY CONFRONTED?
- COULD THIS BE A CHANCE TO GROW AND EVOLVE BY ACKNOWLEDGING AND WORKING THROUGH MY DISCOMFORT?

Your Mirror Is Not Just Reflection, but Opportunity

The people around you are not just characters in your life story; they are powerful reflections of who you are.

Remember, you're the sum of your relationships, not only because you share time with others, but because they reflect parts of you waiting to be embraced, nurtured, and transformed. You don't see people as they are; you often relate to people as you are.

If you want to grow and expand, you must first be willing to see the mirror clearly—not only the parts you love but also the parts you may not yet fully understand. In embracing both, you unlock the power to evolve into the highest version of yourself.

What's the mirror showing you? What are you willing to change in yourself to become the best version of who you're meant to be?

If there are qualities you wish to develop, actively seek to embody them. If there are aspects of yourself you wish to change, commit to doing the inner work required to shift your mindset and habits.

The Impact of Awareness in Your Life

When you embrace awareness, you begin to see the world through a new lens. You no longer react automatically to situations. Instead, you pause, reflect, and choose a response that is in alignment with your values and intentions.

You become the observer of your thoughts and behaviors rather than a passive participant, giving you the power to change your life, one choice at a time.

THE PRINCIPLE OF AWARENESS

The journey of awareness is lifelong and ongoing. But it's the most rewarding journey you can take because it leads to a life that is genuine, aligned, and deeply fulfilling.

And as you continue to grow in awareness, you become empowered to live your fullest life as your greatest, truest self.

13

The Principle of Accountability – Your Pathway to True Success

When most people think of Accountability, one of the first things that comes to mind are reprimands, criticism, and the consequences of not meeting expectations.

It's often associated with finding fault or holding ourselves, or others, up to a standard or some sort of perfection.

But in truth, accountability isn't just about punishment or correction. It's just as much about celebrating the efforts, progress, and accomplishments along the way. It's about honoring the work you do, no matter how big or small, and giving yourself the credit you deserve.

Accountability is the quiet force that says, "I'll do what I said I would do."

But it's also the voice that whispers, "You've done great today, keep going."

When you recognize your efforts *and* hold yourself to a higher standard, you move forward in life with purpose, confidence, and direction.

How often do you value your own efforts with gratitude and appreciation? You spend so much time evaluating your results and setting goals, but do you take time to acknowledge the progress you've made along the way?

Remember, the immaterial things you do—the small, seemingly insignificant actions that no one sees—matter.

Whether it's keeping your word, showing up when you don't feel like it, or simply doing your best with what you have, these actions form the foundation of your character.

And accountability isn't only about the big achievements; it's about owning the little moments, too.

To fully embrace accountability, you must also embrace gratitude. I like to think of the word gratitude as a combination of two key concepts: grateful and attitude. Gratitude isn't just a word. It's a mindset, a way of life. And the way you view the world is directly tied to your attitude.

What kind of attitude do you have today? Is it one of appreciation for the journey you're on, or is it one of frustration, negativity, or self-criticism?

If you're not actively practicing gratitude, what kind of attitude do you bring into your life, your relationships, and your work?

Your attitude is the sum total of your thoughts, feelings, and actions. It shapes how you approach your day, how you view challenges, and how you respond to setbacks.

If your thoughts are focused on what's going wrong, your feelings are filled with doubt or discouragement, and your actions are half-hearted, your results will reflect that.

On the other hand, if you consistently choose an attitude of gratitude—acknowledging your progress, appreciating your efforts, and focusing on what you can control—your results will shift in ways you never thought possible.

You Control the Controllable

One of the greatest sources of frustration comes from focusing on things outside your control.

When you reflect on your thoughts, you may often spend your energy worrying about situations or outcomes you cannot influence, which only drains you mentally and emotionally. Trying to control an outcome only brings worry, doubt, fear, anxiety, or stress.

But true accountability means focusing on what's within your control—your choices, actions, and attitude. You control your mindset, and your character influences your actions.

Celebrate the controllable in your life. Celebrate the moments where you showed up for yourself, even when it was hard. Celebrate the days when you kept your word, when you made an effort, when you stayed consistent. Celebrate the growth that may not always be visible to the world but is deeply felt within you.

Your progress matters, even if no one else sees it.

And most importantly, celebrate you: your efforts, your growth, and your commitment to doing the best you can with what you have.

When you hold yourself accountable to your own standard, rather than comparing yourself to others or chasing perfection, you'll find an inner peace that empowers you to continue the journey with confidence and joy.

It's time to make a change—not in your results, but in your approach.

Let's shift from focusing on what you haven't done to appreciating what you have.

Once you start shifting your focus from external validation to internal celebration, you'll unlock an extraordinary power within yourself. The power of true accountability, not just to others, but most importantly to yourself.

Because when you own your progress, no matter how small, and you celebrate the things you can control, you'll create a life built on a foundation of gratitude, self-love, and empowerment.

This is the energy that will propel you forward, through any obstacle, toward the person you're becoming.

When you do, you'll find your results will come faster and feel more meaningful because you've learned to value the journey, not just the destination.

Accountability is about owning your choices, actions, and results. It's easy to blame others when things don't go as planned, but real growth happens when you take accountability for your efforts and stay focused on your goals. Accountability is the bridge between intention and achievement.

14

The Principle of Responsibility – Embrace Your Decisions and Own Your Journey

Responsibility is often misunderstood. It's not just about carrying burdens or holding yourself accountable for every mistake.

True responsibility is about ownership. It's about being committed to the decisions and choices you make and leaning into the outcome, good or bad.

It's about recognizing that every decision, whether made intentionally or through inaction, carries consequences. Even the decision to do nothing is, in itself, a choice.

How much responsibility are you truly taking for your life?

Every moment, every day, you're making decisions. Some are big—like choosing your career, your relationships, or where to live. Others are small—like how you react to a challenge or spend your time. But no matter how big or small, these decisions are shaping the life you're living right now.

And here is the key: You own them!

You are the architect of your life. Every choice you make builds the person you're becoming and the future you're creating.

Embrace the Outcome: Your Power of Ownership

The first step in taking true responsibility is to embrace the outcome of your decisions, regardless of whether they're the outcomes you hoped for or expected.

When things go wrong, it's easy to shift the blame—to point to circumstances, other people, or to say, "It's just plain, bad luck"

But here's the truth: Your decisions are yours to own, including the outcomes.

Even when things don't go as planned, you're still in control of your response.

This doesn't mean you should feel guilty or beat yourself up over mistakes, but it is an invitation to lean in and learn.

Embrace the outcome, even if it's not perfect. Because with every result, you have the power to pivot, adjust, and grow.

The next time you face an undesirable outcome, ask yourself:

- WHAT CAN I LEARN FROM THIS EXPERIENCE?
- WHAT DECISION LED ME TO THIS POINT?
- HOW CAN I ADJUST MOVING FORWARD?
- WHAT ACTION CAN I TAKE TODAY TO MOVE IN A NEW DIRECTION?

Your Failures Are Not Defeats, They're Opportunities to Evolve

One of the most powerful shifts in perspective you can make is seeing problems, mistakes, and failures not as setbacks, but as opportunities.

Life is full of challenges. You make mistakes, face failures, and encounter obstacles. But these are not signs of defeat; they are merely stepping stones on the path to success. They're actually opportunities to grow and evolve. Now, that's empowerment.

If you embrace the struggle and learn from it, you'll see that each "failure" is a chance to grow, evolve, and get closer to the person you're meant to become.

I want you to think of the times when things didn't go according to plan in your life.

How did you respond? Did you give up? Or did you pivot, adjust, and keep moving forward?

In those moments of struggle, your character is built. You become stronger, more resilient, and more determined to succeed.

When you truly understand the principle of responsibility, you also understand the power of choice. Every decision you make and every action you take shapes your future.

Even when things are not going the way you want, you can always adjust and take new actions. But that choice is yours to make.

How can you take more responsibility in your life today? Is there an area where you've been holding back? Is there something you've been avoiding because of fear or uncertainty? What would it look like if you took ownership and faced that challenge head-on?

What's one small decision you can make to take action and move forward? Have you been blaming external circumstances for where you are in life? What would happen if you stopped waiting for things to change and started taking control of your own path?

Remember, empowerment comes not from waiting for the world to change but from taking full responsibility for your own journey.

It's about making conscious choices, embracing the outcomes—good and bad—and knowing that no setback is permanent as long as you don't quit. You can always pivot. You can always learn, grow, and adjust. The power is in your hands.

So, I encourage you to take a step back today and reflect on your own journey.

Are you fully owning the decisions you've made? Are you embracing the outcomes of your choices, even if they don't look like what you expected? Are you ready to see problems and failures as stepping stones to success?

Embrace your responsibility. It's your life, your journey, and your destiny. Own it, lean in, and move forward. Because the power to change and grow is always within you.

15

The Principle of Expectations – Your Journey, Your Light, Your Purpose

As we explore the final principle of the i.C.A.A.R.E. Mindset—Expectations—let's begin by reflecting on what it truly means to expect something in life. Expectations are not just goals or distant aspirations.

They're the mile markers that guide you on your journey, the dots that, when connected, reveal the unique path of your life.

Steve Jobs famously said:

> You cannot connect the dots looking forward; you can only connect them looking backwards. So, you have to trust that the dots will somehow connect in your future. You have to trust in something. Your gut, destiny, life, karma, whatever. Because believing in the dots will connect down the road and will give you the confidence to follow your heart, even when it leads you off the well-worn path, and that will make all the difference.

This quote holds an essential truth: Life is not linear. The journey toward our highest self isn't always clear when we're walking it. The dots are not always visible in the moment.

But when you look back and reflect on the experiences that've shaped you, you begin to see how every step, every struggle, every triumph, and every mistake was part of a bigger picture.

Our journey is a series of connected dots, each moment leading you closer to who you're meant to become.

Your Life Is a Masterclass

As you go through life, you're not just living out experiences. You're learning, growing, and evolving from them.

Your life is a masterclass—a continuous lesson in personal growth, purpose, and self-discovery.

And just as any great teacher would tell you, it's the mistakes, setbacks, and challenges that often hold the most valuable lessons.

The beauty of connecting the dots in hindsight is that you come to realize something profound: Today's ceiling is tomorrow's floor.

The difficulties you face today are simply the foundation upon which you'll build tomorrow. The struggles that seem insurmountable today will eventually be the very ground you stand on as you rise to greater heights.

This concept shifts your perspective. It reframes challenges not as obstacles to your happiness, but as necessary stepping stones on your way to fulfillment.

So, no matter where you are on your journey—whether you're at the top of your game or in the midst of a struggle—know that you're exactly where you're supposed to be. Today's challenges are the foundation of your future success.

The Fear of Your Own Light

When you were young, you'd sing songs about letting your light shine, and yet, as you grow older, you often dim that light. You become afraid of it. You worry that shining too brightly will make others uncomfortable, or that your light will reveal too much of who you are.

But as Marianne Williamson reiterates in *A Return to Love:*

> Our deepest fear is not that we are inadequate. Our deepest fear is that we are powerful beyond measure. It is our light, not our darkness, that most frightens us.

Why are we so afraid of shining? Why, as we grow older, do we fear stepping into our full potential? Why do we allow our doubts, insecurities, and fears to control us?

Williamson continues:

> You are a child of God. Playing small does not serve the world. There is nothing enlightened about shrinking so that other people won't feel insecure around you. We are all meant to shine, as children do.

Let this be your reminder: You were born to shine.

The world doesn't need more people playing small, hiding their gifts, or dimming their light. The world needs you fully expressed, powerful, radiant, and unapologetically and imperfectly you.

Your light is meant to be shared.

When you allow yourself to shine, you not only liberate yourself, but also you give those around you permission to do the same.

The Gift of Your Purpose

The most profound way to embrace your light is to understand your purpose—the "beliefs" behind everything you do.

Mark Twain once said, "The two most important days of your life are the day you were born and the day you discovered why."

Finding your purpose isn't about a destination; it's about discovery.

It's about connecting the dots that have led you to this point and realizing that every experience, every challenge, every success, and every failure has been part of the greater plan to reveal your true self.

It's about trusting that your purpose is not a destination, but a journey—one that evolves, grows, and deepens as you move forward.

The expectation you set for yourself is not merely about achieving goals. It's about connecting with your purpose and letting that belief guide every action, every decision, and every moment.

Live Fully and Shine Brightly

Are you ready to step into your light? Are you ready to trust in your journey, to embrace the mistakes, the challenges, and the achievements, understanding that every single one of them is part of your path? Are you ready to connect the dots and see your life for what it truly is—a masterclass in personal growth, filled with lessons that shape the extraordinary person you're becoming?

Joseph Campbell profoundly states, "The cave you fear to enter holds the very treasure you seek."

Your light is not something to fear. It's the gift that will illuminate your path and the path of others.

Take this moment to reflect:

- WHAT DOTS IN YOUR LIFE HAVE ALREADY CONNECTED TO BRING YOU HERE?
- WHAT EXPERIENCES HAVE SHAPED YOU INTO THE PERSON YOU ARE TODAY?
- WHAT'S THE ONE THING YOU'VE BEEN AFRAID TO EMBRACE ABOUT YOURSELF, AND HOW CAN YOU BEGIN TO LET IT SHINE?

You are stronger than your biggest worry, doubt, fear, anxiety, stress, or setback. You're more powerful than you realize. Your light is meant to shine, and as you let it shine, you give others the freedom to do the same.

You're here for a reason. Your journey matters, your light matters, and your purpose is waiting to be fully embraced.

Trust in the dots that will connect and keep you moving forward with the confidence that you're exactly where you meant to be.

Setting clear expectations, the standards for yourself, is a powerful way to grow. When you define what you expect of yourself, whether it's honesty, effort, or kindness—you set a standard for how you want to live.

Expectations give you clarity, direction, and a sense of purpose as you work toward your goals.

Shine bright. Live fully. The world is waiting for you to step into your greatness.

PART IV:
THE ASCENSION – LIVING OUT YOUR GREATEST YOU

Living intentionally, leaving impact, and becoming a beacon of purpose

The Principles of the i.C.A.A.R.E. Mindset –
A Daily Practice

The i.C.A.A.R.E. Mindset is about growth, self-reflection, and human potential. It's a way to approach life with confidence and integrity, knowing that each day brings opportunities to get better, learn, and achieve more.

Here's how you can apply the i.C.A.A.R.E. principles every day:

- **CELEBRATE YOUR INDIVIDUALITY**
  REFLECT ON YOUR UNIQUENESS AND STRENGTHS AND LET THEM SHINE.

- **STRENGTHEN COMMUNICATION**
  FOCUS ON HOW YOU CONNECT WITH OTHERS— LISTEN, SPEAK HONESTLY, AND BUILD TRUST.

- **GROW YOUR AWARENESS**
  REFLECT ON YOUR ACTIONS, EMOTIONS, AND THOUGHTS TO SEE HOW THEY SHAPE YOUR LIFE.

- **EMBRACE ACCOUNTABILITY**
  FOLLOW THROUGH ON YOUR COMMITMENTS AND ALIGN YOUR ACTIONS WITH YOUR VALUES.

- **HONOR RESPONSIBILITY**
  TAKE OWNERSHIP OF YOUR CHOICES AND FOCUS ON WHAT YOU CAN DO TO MOVE FORWARD.

- **SET CLEAR EXPECTATIONS**
  DEFINE WHAT YOU WANT FROM YOURSELF, AND LET THOSE EXPECTATIONS GUIDE YOUR GROWTH.

Confidence comes from knowing who you are, reflecting on where you're going, and taking intentional action every day.

When you live by the i.C.A.A.R.E. Mindset, you're not just setting goals. You're building the habits, relationships, and mindset to achieve them. You've got what it takes to grow, thrive, and succeed. It all starts with you.

16

Your Greatest You– The Power of the Interconnected Principles

As you reflect on the principles of the i.C.A.A.R.E. Mindset, it is important to understand that they're not isolated concepts—they work together, interwoven into the fabric of your daily life.

Every action, every decision, every thought, and every relationship is deeply influenced by these principles. The way these principles play out in your life shapes your self-image, your personal relationships, your physical health, your mental well-being, your personal growth, your personal finances, and ultimately, your sense of fulfillment and purpose.

Now, let's take a deeper look at how the principles of having an i.C.A.A.R.E. Mindset intertwine.

i.C.A.A.R.E. About My Self-Image

At the heart of everything is who you believe you are, your self-image. This is your foundation. The way you see yourself determines how you live, how you make choices, and how you interact with the world. Your self-image is either empowering you or limiting you. The principle of individuality in the i.C.A.A.R.E. Mindset invites you to reflect on your truest and highest expression of self.

What would it look like to wake up every day motivated and inspired to live your full potential? When you see yourself as the highest version of you—whole, capable, worthy, and powerful—you align your actions with that vision.

Your self-image becomes the lens through which you make all decisions. This clarity enables you to live a fulfilling life, because you know who you are at the core, and you're committed to being that person.

The better you see yourself, the better you can show up for others, leading to a life filled with purpose and satisfaction.

i.C.A.A.R.E. About My Personal Relationships

The i.C.A.A.R.E. Mindset also speaks directly to your relationships—both intimate and social. But before you can fully engage with others, you must first develop a strong relationship with yourself.

You cannot give what you do not have!

Think about the people you interact with the most—your spouse, significant other, family, friends, and colleagues. They are your K.P.I.s – the "Key People Influencers" who shape your life's direction and provide you with invaluable feedback.

The principle of Communication in the i.C.A.A.R.E. Mindset reminds us that effective communication is a foundational life skill in any relationship. It's not only about what you say, but how you listen, how you engage, and how your actions align with your words.

When you actively listen, you build trust, deepen connections, and create an environment where people feel safe and valued.

In relationships, this principle also emphasizes the importance of accountability—you own your actions, contributions, and the impact you have on others.

Be the change you wish to see, whether it's in your personal relationships, your friendships, or your family dynamics.

When you take full responsibility for your relationships and the role you play in them, you transform your life and the lives of those around you.

i.C.A.A.R.E. About My Physical Health

Your body is the vessel that carries you through this life, and treating it with respect is a direct reflection of how much you value yourself.

The principle of Awareness in the i.C.A.A.R.E. Mindset invites you to bring conscious attention to how you treat your body, your nutrition, and your physical well-being.

When you're mindful of what you put into your body—through nutrition, exercise, and rest—you empower yourself to show up fully in every aspect of your life. This self-care becomes a habit that increases your energy, boosts your confidence, and enhances your overall sense of well-being.

A healthy body fuels a healthy mind, and when your physical health is in alignment with your personal values, your ability to live your best life expands exponentially.

i.C.A.A.R.E. About My Mental Well-Being

In this fast-paced world, it is easy to forget the importance of nurturing your mental health. Your thoughts are powerful, and the principle of Responsibility in the i.C.A.A.R.E. Mindset reminds you that you have full ownership of your mental landscape.

You can choose to let negative thoughts take root, or you can take responsibility for nurturing a mindset that serves you.

Your mental well-being isn't just about managing stress or dealing with anxiety. It's about feeding your mind with the right inputs.

What you read, what you listen to, what you watch—all of these affect your thoughts and, ultimately, your actions.

By engaging your higher intellectual faculties, your SuperPowers, and drawing on universal laws like the law of vibration and law of polarity, you can create a mindset that attracts positivity, growth, and opportunity.

And when you train your mind to think positively, to reflect critically, and to engage with life purposefully, your mindset will reflect the high standards you set for yourself.

i.C.A.A.R.E. About My Personal Growth and Development

You must continually nurture your talents, gifts, purpose, and passions. This area of your life is where you truly become the greatest version of yourself.

What you do during your personal growth and development is how you utilize your time.

As I've heard Jay Shetty wisely say:

> Time is free, but it is priceless. You can't own it, but you can use it. You can't keep it, but you can spend it. And once it's lost, you can never get it back. It's our choice how we use our time. Life and time are our best two teachers. Life teaches us to make good use of time, and time teaches us the value of life.

Put more life in your time! Where are you investing your time in personal growth? Are you prioritizing learning? Are you committing to self-improvement?

Remember, every day is an opportunity to grow, to stretch yourself beyond your comfort zone, to explore new opportunities, and to become a better version of who you were yesterday.

i.C.A.A.R.E. About My Personal Finances

The way you perceive money speaks volumes about your paradigm—your beliefs, thoughts, and behaviors surrounding wealth. You may have heard these sayings:

- MONEY DOESN'T GROW ON TREES.
- MONEY IS THE ROOT OF ALL EVIL.
- GOOD THINGS COME TO THOSE WHO WAIT.
- BETTER TO BE SAFE THAN SORRY.

These are beliefs ingrained in many minds. These sayings, while common, can limit your potential for financial growth.

The i.C.A.A.R.E. Mindset invites you to examine your relationship with money.

Do you see money as a tool for freedom and opportunity, or do you see it as something scarce or evil? Money goes where it is invited and stays where it is welcomed. Remember, money is a tool, not a measure of your worth.

If you can change your mindset about money, you can attract it into your life. Your thoughts about money directly influence your financial reality.

What amount of money would bring you peace and freedom?

Bob Proctor stated:

> The Law of Compensation is in direct ratio to the need of what you do, your ability to do it, and the difficulty to replace you. And when you do the second thing extremely well, it takes care of the other two; the need of what you do, and the difficulty to replace you.

Visualize the financial goals that will provide you with the comfort and security to live the life you've always dreamed of.

The principles of responsibility and accountability remind you that you're in charge of your finances. Every choice you make today—whether it's how you spend, invest, or save—is a reflection of your financial mindset.

Take ownership of your wealth-building journey and set clear goals to create the financial future you desire.

Living from the Inside Out

Are you living from the inside out, where your choices, values, and actions align with your deepest truth? Or are you living from the outside in, where external factors dictate how you think, feel, and act?

The i.C.A.A.R.E. Mindset encourages you to take control of your life and live authentically.

Your Self-Image, Relationships, Physical Health, Mental Well-Being, Personal Growth, and Personal Finances are all reflections of the principles you choose to live by.

As you integrate these principles, you align your actions with your highest self, and in doing so, you create a life of freedom, abundance, and fulfillment.

17

A Message about Life – Stay Humble, Stay Hungry, Stay True to You

As you walk through life, applying these principles will guide you toward becoming the greatest version of yourself.

Here's a message I want to leave with you—a simple yet powerful framework for living a life that's aligned with your purpose, your potential, and your truth.

Stay Humble

Gratitude is the key to staying grounded along your journey. It helps you see how far you've come, appreciate what you have, and stay focused on what truly matters.

Stay Hungry

Personal growth begins with curiosity. Stay curious about who you are, what you're capable of, and what you have to offer the world. Never stop asking questions, exploring, and seeking to grow into the person you're meant to be.

Stay True to You

The most powerful thing you can do is be yourself. At your core, you already know who you are and what you're capable of. Stay connected to that truth and don't let anyone, or anything, convince you that you can't be, do, or have what you truly desire.

Henry Ford has a great thought-provoking quote: "If you think you can or you think you can't, you're most certainly right."

The world is full of opinions, but the only voice that truly matters is your own. If there's something you deeply want, if there is a dream in your heart:

- IT'S MEANT FOR YOU.

- YOUR BELIEF IN YOURSELF IS STRONGER THAN ANYONE'S DOUBT.

- NO ONE ELSE GETS TO DECIDE WHAT YOU CAN OR CAN'T DO.

- YOU ARE THE CREATOR OF YOUR OWN LIFE.

Turning Awareness into Power, Living Boldly, and Aligning Values with Mindset and Character

Unlocking your greatest you means living a life of freedom, abundance, and fulfillment. It's about being true to who you are, following your passions, and creating a life that feels meaningful and aligned with your deepest values—from the inside out.

You're capable of more than you realize. Your potential is limitless. The world is waiting for what only you can bring.

When you live in alignment with the principles in the i.C.A.A.R.E. Mindset, you're stepping into your highest self.

Conclusion

The Mirror – Seeing the Reflection of Who You Are

Closing the journey with clarity, confidence, and courage

Reflection of Your Own Values and Self-Worth

This reflection is for you to embrace this content to Empower, Engage, Evolve, and Lead (E3L) every day. Repeat these affirmations daily to live the life you truly desire.

Because i.C.A.A.R.E., I see the incredible person you're becoming.

Because i.C.A.A.R.E., I know that inside you is a spark—your individuality—that no one else in this world has. It's the light you were born with, the one that reminds you of your strength, your talents, and your infinite potential waiting to be unleashed.

Because i.C.A.A.R.E., I want you to know that your voice matters, your dreams matter, and your journey matters. Even when it feels like no one sees your struggles or understands your hopes, I see you. I see the resilience it takes to keep showing up, the Courage it takes to dream bigger, and the hunger in your heart to live a life that truly feels like yours.

Because i.C.A.A.R.E., I want you to stay Curious about what's possible. To keep asking yourself, "Who can I become? How can I grow? What do I truly want?" Let your curiosity guide you; it's how you'll discover the incredible things you're capable of.

Because i.C.A.A.R.E., I want you to live with Gratitude, even on the hard days. Gratitude will remind you of the beauty in the little things, the lessons in the challenges, and the progress you're making step by step.

Because i.C.A.A.R.E., I believe in your ability to take ownership of your life. You're not a passenger in your story; you're the driver. Take Responsibility for your choices, your growth, and your future. You're powerful, even in moments when you feel lost or unsure.

Because i.C.A.A.R.E., I want you to trust yourself. Trust your heart, your instincts, and the dreams that make your soul light up. Stay true to who you are and never let anyone tell you that you can't be, do, or have what you know is meant for you.

Because i.C.A.A.R.E., I want you to live a life that feels deeply fulfilling—a life that reflects the truest and highest expression of who you are. The freedom, abundance, and joy you're searching for won't come from outside of you; it will come from within when you align with your purpose and stay true to your heart.

CONCLUSION

Every time you look in the mirror, every time you face a challenge, and every time you take one more step toward your dreams, I want you to remind yourself:

- STAY HUMBLE
- STAY HUNGRY
- STAY TRUE TO YOU
- DREAM BIG
- TAKE ACTION
- BE UNAPOLOGETICALLY AND IMPERFECTLY YOU
- SOMEONE ELSE'S OPINION OF YOU IS NONE OF YOUR BUSINESS
- I.C.A.A.R.E.

The life you desire, the life you know in your heart is possible, is waiting for you.

Never stop striving to live at the truest and highest expression of your God-given talents, gifts, and passions. Live a life with meaning and purpose that brings freedom, abundance, and fulfillment, in alignment with who you are from the inside out.

About the Author

Joseph G. Motley

Speaker | Coach | Trainer | Author | Leader of Mindset and Character

Joseph G. Motley, affectionately known by many as "Coach Mot," is more than a coach; he's a transformational leader with a calling to awaken purpose, ignite potential, and shape powerful lives from the inside out.

Born and raised in a small blue-collar town by a devoted single mother alongside his three sisters, Coach Mot's early life was rooted in love, faith, and resilience. Although accepted into college after high school, he made the bold decision to forge his own path, stepping into the workforce to pursue what many would define as "the American Dream." A decent job. Good benefits. Two-and-a-half kids and a picket fence, a loving wife, yearly vacations. The works.

But something deeper stirred within him—a persistent whisper of unfulfillment that challenged him to ask: "Am I really living the dream? And if so, whose dream is it?"

That soul-stirring question led Coach Mot to one of his favorite life-defining truths: "What shall it profit a man if he gains the whole world, but loses his own soul?" From that moment, his life's journey transformed. He shifted from chasing external validation to cultivating internal value, laying the foundation for a life led by purpose, not possessions.

Coach Mot immersed himself in the world of personal development, studying the insights of the world's greatest thought leaders, coaches, and visionaries. Blending his real-life experiences with timeless principles, he authored *Unlocking Your Greatest You:*

Turning Awareness into Power, Living Boldly, and Aligning Values with Mindset and Character—a practical roadmap for inner transformation and lifelong growth.

With nearly four decades of professional experience in leadership roles within the manufacturing industry, Coach Mot's journey is as blue-collar as it is breakthrough. His career, however, didn't stop at the workplace. His passion for youth and leadership took root on the basketball court, where for over thirty years he mentored elite student-athletes as an assistant basketball coach in public and college preparatory private schools, helping them win multiple championships, but more importantly, helping the students develop their mindset and character far beyond the game.

His dedication to growth and excellence led him to earn certifications as a Certified Professional Coach (CPC) and an Energy Leadership Index Master Practitioner (ELI-MP) through the International Professional Excellence in Coaching (IPEC), an accredited institution of the International Coach Federation (IFC). Further expanding his influence, he became a certified speaker, coach, and trainer through the John C. Maxwell Leadership Certification Program, equipped and authorized to teach global leadership content that transforms individuals, teams, and organizations.

Whether he's mentoring on the court, speaking to communities, or consulting with professionals and students alike, Coach Mot embodies the belief that we were not created just to survive, but to thrive, create, and live in alignment with who we were born to be.

His message is simple, but powerful: You are not broken. You are becoming. Your greatest you is already within—waiting to be unlocked.

This is your invitation. To think differently. To live intentionally. To rise boldly.

www.ingramcontent.com/pod-product-compliance
Lightning Source LLC
Chambersburg PA
CBHW061233070526
44584CB00030B/4097